A Pet's Life

Guinea Pigs

Anita Ganeri

Heinemann
LIBRARY

www.heinemann.co.uk/library
Visit our website to find out more information about **Heinemann Library** books.

To order:
☎ Phone 44 (0) 1865 888066
🖹 Send a fax to 44 (0) 1865 314091
💻 Visit the Heinemann Bookshop at www.heinemann.co.uk/library to browse our catalogue and order online.

First published in Great Britain by Heinemann Library, Halley Court, Jordan Hill, Oxford OX2 8EJ, part of Harcourt Education.
Heinemann is a registered trademark of Harcourt Education Ltd.

Editorial: Jilly Attwood and Claire Throp
Design: Richard Parker and Tinstar Design Limited (www.tinstar.co.uk)
Picture Research: Rosie Garai
Production: Séverine Ribierre

Originated by Dot Gradations
Printed and bound in China by South China Printing Company

ISBN 0 431 17761 9
07 06 05 04 03
10 9 8 7 6 5 4 3 2 1

British Library Cataloguing in Publication Data
Ganeri, Anita
    Guinea Pigs – (A Pet's Life)
    636.9'3592
A full catalogue record for this book is available from the British Library.

Acknowledgements
The publishers would like to thank the following for permission to reproduce photographs: Mark Farrell **pp. 9, 13, 27**; RSPCA **pp. 10, 24** (Angela Hampton); Tudor Photography **pp. 4, 8, 11, 12, 14, 15, 16, 17, 18, 19, 20, 21, 23, 25**; Warren Photographic **pp. 5, 6, 7, 22, 26** (Jane Burton)

Cover photograph reproduced with permission of Alamy/Maximillian Weinzeir.

The publishers would like to thank Pippa Bush of the RSPCA for her assistance in the preparation of this book.

Every effort has been made to contact copyright holders of any material reproduced in this book. Any omissions will be rectified in subsequent printings if notice is given to the publishers.

Disclaimer
All the Internet addresses (URLs) given in this book were valid at the time of going to press. However, due to the dynamic nature of the Internet, some addresses may have changed, or sites may have ceased to exist since publication. While the author and publishers regret any inconvenience this may cause readers, no responsibility for any such changes can be accepted by either the author or the publishers.

RSPCA Trading Limited (which pays all its taxable profits to the RSPCA, Registered Charity No. 219099) receives a royalty for every copy of this book sold by Heinemann Library. Details of the royalties payable to RSPCA Trading Limited can be obtained by writing to the Publisher, Heinemann Library, Halley Court, Jordan Hill, Oxford, OX2 8EJ. For the purposes of the Charities Act 1992 no further seller of this book shall be deemed to be a commercial participator with the RSPCA. RSPCA name and logo are trademarks of the RSPCA used by Heinemann Library under licence from RSPCA Trading Ltd.

Contents

Any words appearing in the text in bold,
like this, are explained in the Glossary.

What is a guinea pig?

Guinea pigs are very popular pets. There are many different kinds and colours of guinea pigs. Some guinea pigs have short hair. Some have long hair.

A short-haired guinea pig is best for a first-time pet owner.

Here you can see the different parts of a guinea pig's body and what each part is used for.

Fur. Long-haired guinea pigs need brushing every day to keep their fur free from tangles.

Ears for hearing.

Tiny tail.

Beady eyes.

Whiskers for sensing.

Claws for walking and **grooming**.

Long front teeth for **gnawing**.

Guinea pig babies

A mother guinea pig has about four babies in a **litter**. The babies are born with lots of fur and with their eyes open.

The baby guinea pigs drink their mother's milk.

The babies are old enough to leave their mother when they are about six weeks old. Then they are ready to become pets.

A female guinea pig can have 20 babies a year. So it is best to keep males and females apart.

Your pet guinea pigs

Guinea pigs make wonderful pets and are quite easy to keep. But you must be a good pet owner and care for them properly.

Your guinea pigs will depend on you for all their needs.

Your guinea pigs need food and water every day. If you are going on holiday, ask a friend or neighbour to look after your pets.

Write a list of what your friend should do and leave it by the guinea pig house.

Choosing your guinea pigs

You can buy guinea pigs from good pet shops or guinea pig breeders. **Animal shelters** often need good homes for guinea pigs.

Guinea pigs like company. It is unkind to keep just one as a pet. Choose two males or two females from the same **litter**.

Pick plump guinea pigs with shiny coats. Check that their ears and eyes are clean, and that their teeth are not too long.

A healthy guinea pig should be lively and alert.

11

Your guinea pigs' house

Your guinea pigs need a large house to live in. It should have a living space with a **wire mesh** front and a sleeping space with a solid door.

Put a layer of wood shavings on the floor, and a good pile of hay for bedding.

Keep the house outside and raised off the ground. In winter, you can move it inside your home, or into a shed or garage.

For two guinea pigs, the house should measure at least 120 x 60 x 45 cm.

Welcome home

You can bring your guinea pigs home in a small cat-carrying basket or a sturdy box. Leave them for a while so that they can settle into their new home.

Make sure that the carrying box has holes in it so that your guinea pigs can breathe.

Guinea pigs are quite timid. Be gentle
when you pick your pet up. Put one hand
under its bottom and the other hand
around its shoulders.

Stroke your guinea
pig gently and make
a fuss of it.

Play time

Guinea pigs need lots of space to play and exercise. Make them an outside run in the garden. In cold or wet weather, an indoor **pen** is best.

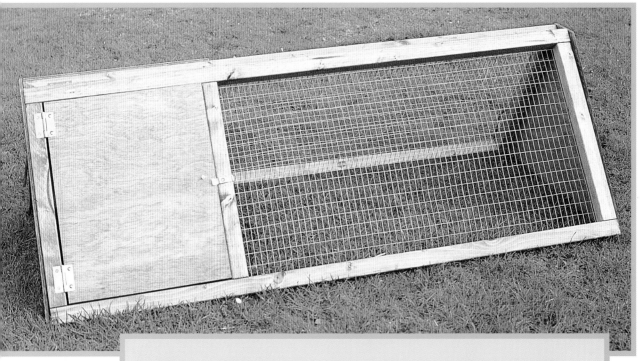

The outdoor run should have **wire mesh** sides to stop your pets escaping.

Guinea pigs love to play hide and seek. Put some logs, rocks and piles of hay in the run for your pets to explore.

Don't forget to put some food and water in the run.

17

Feeding time

You can buy special guinea pig food from a pet shop. Guinea pigs also like to eat chopped fresh fruit and vegetables.

Your guinea pigs need lots of **vitamin C**. They can get this from good hay, greenstuff, raw apples, carrots and cabbage leaves.

You should feed your guinea pigs every morning and evening. Put the food in heavy bowls which will not tip over.

Make sure that your guinea pigs have fresh drinking water every day. Give them a **drip feeder**.

Cleaning

You can help to keep your guinea pigs healthy by keeping their house clean. Take away any wet bedding, old food and **droppings** every day.

Put in some fresh wood shavings and lots of hay for bedding.

Once a week, empty the house and give it a good clean. You also need to wash out the **drip feeder** and food bowls. Don't forget to clean out the outside run.

At least four times a year, give the house a thorough scrub. Leave it to dry before you put your pets back in.

Growing up

Guinea pigs grow up quickly. When a male guinea pig is fully grown, it will weigh about the same as a large bag of sugar (1 kg). Female guinea pigs are slightly smaller.

Male guinea pigs are bigger than females.

Guinea pigs like to talk a lot. They squeak, tweet, chatter and chirrup, and whistle. You will soon get to know what your guinea pig means.

If your guinea pig whistles, it means that it is hungry or thirsty.

Healthy guinea pigs

Your guinea pigs will stay healthy if you take care of them. If your pets look unwell, take them to a vet straightaway.

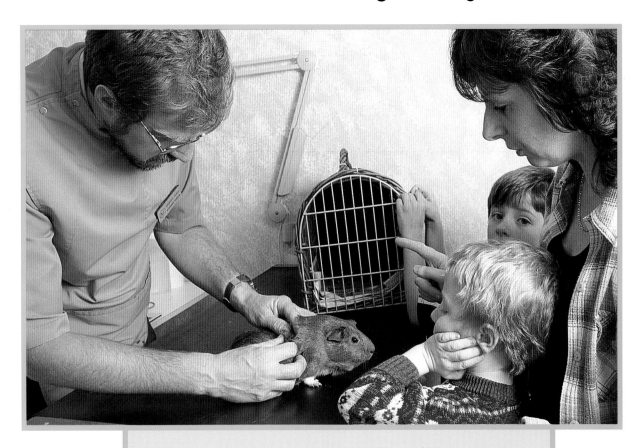

 If your guinea pig is not eating, seems tired or starts sneezing, it may be ill.

A guinea pig's front teeth and claws can grow too long. If they do, it will not be able to eat properly. A vet can trim their claws.

Give your pets a wooden **gnawing** block to wear their teeth down.

Old age

If you look after your guinea pigs, they may live for up to seven years. Guinea pigs hate the cold. You need to make sure they are warm, especially in winter.

As your guinea pig gets older, check it every day to make sure that it is healthy.

It can be very upsetting when your pets die. Try not to be too sad. Just remember the happy times you shared together.

Caring for your guinea pigs will help you learn how to treat animals properly.

Useful tips

- Always wash your hands before and after touching your pets.

- Guinea pigs **groom** themselves. But you need to brush long-haired guinea pigs every day to stop their fur getting tangled. Use a soft toothbrush or a baby's hairbrush.

- If your pet holds its head to one side and cannot walk in a straight line, it may have an ear **infection**. Take it to a vet.

- If your guinea pigs start pulling out each other's hair, it means that they are bored. Make sure that they get plenty of exercise. If your guinea pig is pulling its own hair out, it may have **mange**. Take it to a vet.

- Don't let guinea pigs run around your house. They may chew electric cables.

Fact file

- Wild guinea pigs live in South America.

- Guinea pigs are named after Guiana, the South American country in which they were found.

- Guinea pigs are rodents. They belong to the same group of animals as hamsters, squirrels and mice.

- Male guinea pigs are called boars and females are called sows, just like real pigs.

- Adult guinea pigs need about 50–80 g of dry food a day, plus 100 g of fresh fruit and vegetables and lots of hay.

- Guinea pigs can catch colds from humans.

Glossary

animal shelters places where lost or unwanted animals can be looked after and found new homes

drip feeder a bottle that lets water slowly drip out. It is fixed to the guinea pig's house.

droppings guinea pigs' poo

gnawing chewing and biting

grooming gently brushing and cleaning your guinea pig's fur. Guinea pigs also groom themselves.

infection an illness

litter a group of baby guinea pigs

mange a nasty skin disease

pen a large, open box for your guinea pigs to play in indoors

vitamin C goodness from food which guinea pigs need to stay healthy

wire mesh a sheet of wire with holes in it

More information

Books to read

A First Look at Animals: Pets, Claire Watts (Two-Can Publishing, 2000)

My Pet: Guinea pig, Honor Head (Belitha Press, 2000)

Read and Wonder: I Love Guinea Pigs, Dick King-Smith & Anita Jeram (Walker Books, 1994)

The Official RSPCA Pet Guide: Care for your Guinea Pig (HarperCollins, 1990)

Websites

www.rspca.org.uk
>   The website of The Royal Society for the Prevention of Cruelty to Animals in Britain.

www.pethealthcare.co.uk
>   Information about keeping and caring for first pets.

www.petnet.com.au
>   Information about being a good pet owner.

Index

Titles in the *A Pet's Life* series include:

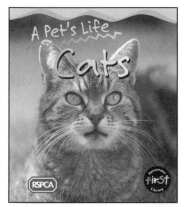

Hardback   0 431 17762 7

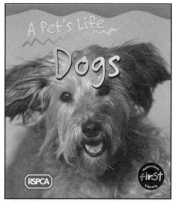

Hardback   0 431 17764 3

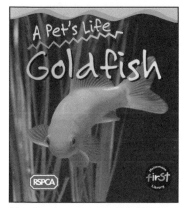

Hardback   0 431 17765 1

Hardback   0 431 17761 9

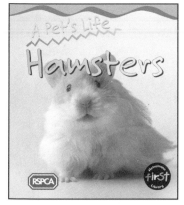

Hardback   0 431 17763 5

Hardback   0 431 17760 0

Find out about the other titles in this series on our website www.heinemann.co.uk/library